BEETLES

BEETLES

by Sylvia A. Johnson

Photographs by Isao Kishida

A Lerner Natural Science Book

Lerner Publications Company ▪ Minneapolis

Sylvia A. Johnson, Series Editor

Translation of original text by Kay Kushino

Additional photographs by Namao Kikaku, page 37 (right), and Klaus Paysan, pages 40 and 41.

The publisher wishes to thank Ronald L. Huber, Entomologist, The Science Museum of Minnesota, for his assistance in the preparation of this book.

The glossary on page 46 gives definitions and pronunciations of words shown in **bold type** in the text. A note on beetle families appears on the following page.

LIBRARY OF CONGRESS CATALOGING IN PUBLICATION DATA

Johnson, Sylvia A.
  Beetles.

    (A Lerner natural science book)
    Adaptation of: Kabutomushi/by Isao Kishida.
    Includes index.
    Summary: Introduces members of the beetle family, discussing their development, environment, and life cycle.
    1. Beetles—Juvenile literature. [1. Beetles] I. Kishida, Isao, ill. II. Kishida, Isao. Kabutomushi. III. Title. IV. Series.
    QL576.2.J63   595.76   82-7230
    ISBN 0-8225-1476-1(lib. bdg.)   AACR2

This edition first published 1982 by Lerner Publications Company.
Text copyright © 1982 by Lerner Publications Company.
Photographs copyright © 1971 by Isao Kishida.
Adapted from BEETLES copyright © 1971 by Isao Kishida.
English language rights arranged by Kurita-Bando Literary Agency for Akane Shobo Publishers, Tokyo, Japan.

International Standard Book Number: 0-8225-1476-1
Library of Congress Catalog Card Number: 82-7230

  3   4   5   6   7   8   9   10   90   89   88   87   86   85   84

This black beetle belongs to the large family of scarab beetles.

Spotted ladybugs crawling up the stem of a garden plant; fireflies flashing signals on a summer night; shiny brown June bugs buzzing around a lighted lamp. These familiar insects are only a few of the more than 200,000 kinds of beetles that live in our world.

Beetles come in many shapes and sizes, and they have many different ways of life. But all beetles have the same basic body structure and develop in the same way. Let's take a look at these fascinating insects.

Left and opposite:
Eggs of a scarab bee-
tle, enlarged many
times their actual
size

A beetle begins its life inside an egg like the ones pictured on these two pages. This egg is the first stage in a complicated process of development called **metamorphosis.** Like ants, butterflies, and a few other kinds of insects, beetles go through four separate stages as they develop into adults. Each of these stages is very different from all the others.

The first stage of metamorphosis begins when a female beetle lays her eggs. Some kinds of beetles lay as many as 2,000 eggs at one time, while others have only a single egg. The eggs are laid in many different places. Some beetles bury their eggs in the soil. Others attach them to plants or put them into holes in the bark of a tree. One group, known as dung beetles, hide their eggs inside balls of animal manure, or dung. Here they will be warm and protected until they are ready to hatch.

6

Opposite: A scarab beetle larva that has just hatched. *Right:* The larvae of scarab beetles have curved, C-shaped bodies.

When the soft covering of a beetle egg breaks open, a tiny wormlike creature emerges. This **larva** or **grub** is the second stage in the insect's development. The larva looks very different from an adult beetle. It has no wings, and its body is made up of many segments or sections. Some beetle larvae are long and slender, while others have fat, curved bodies. The larvae of some species have six legs, just like adult beetles. Other larvae have no real legs at all and move around by wiggling their bodies.

Opposite: Along each side of a larva's body is a row of breathing holes, or spiracles. *Left:* This scarab larva is equipped with large mandibles, curved mouthparts used in collecting food.

Even though the larvae of different beetle species vary in appearance, they are alike in many ways. One thing that they have in common is an enormous appetite. Larvae eat constantly, and each species has its own special kind of food. Many beetle larvae eat parts of plants or decayed plant material in the soil. Other larvae are hunters and feed on small insects that they capture. Some eat the bodies of dead animals or animal dung.

Because they eat so much, larvae grow rapidly. Their bodies get bigger, but their skins do not stretch and expand. At least three times during the larval stage, the beetle grubs shed their skins and grow new ones. This process is called **molting**.

Opposite: These scarab beetle pupae have found shelter in holes dug in the ground. *Above:* As a pupa develops, the body of the adult beetle can be seen taking shape inside the pupal shell.

When a larva has grown to its full size, it is time for it to enter the next stage of metamorphosis and become a **pupa.** The larva finds a protected place, such as a hole in the ground or in a tree. There it remains quiet while a hard shell forms over its body. Inside the shell, the body of the larva changes into the very different body of an adult beetle. This change usually takes about a month. At the end of that time, the fully developed beetle is ready to emerge from the pupal shell.

Above and opposite: An adult scarab beetle emerging from its pupal shell

The pictures on these two pages show a horned scarab beetle emerging from its pupal shell. The hard shell cracks open, and the beetle slowly pushes its way out (above). Even after the beetle has completely emerged, part of the pupal shell remains wrapped around the large, forked horn on its head (opposite).

At first, the outer covering of the beetle's body is soft and flexible, but it soon becomes hard and firm. The scarab's dazzling white color gradually turns to brown and then to a shiny black.

Twenty-four hours after leaving the pupal shell, the beetle will look like all the other adults of its species. Its metamorphosis will be complete.

Male scarab beetles of this species *(Allomyrina dichotoma)* have large forked horns on their heads and smaller curved horns on the middle sections of their bodies.

After its development is complete, a beetle is ready for its first flight. Most beetles are not graceful fliers, and they do not move very fast. Their bodies are heavy, and they fly using only one pair of wings. During flight, a beetle's front

18

wings stay in one position. They help to keep the insect balanced, and they provide lift, something like the wings of an airplane. But only the hind wings move up and down, raising the beetle into the air and keeping it aloft.

A beetle must spread out its front wings in order to unfold the hind wings hidden underneath.

The way in which a beetle uses its wings is unique in the world of insects. The front wings play only a small role during flight. Their main function is to serve as covers or cases for the hind wings while the beetle is at rest. These protective front wings have a special name; they are called **elytra**.

When a beetle is sitting still, as in the picture on the opposite page, the elytra cover most of the back of its body. The two hard front wings come together neatly in a straight line down the middle of the back. The insect's thin, transparent hind wings are folded up and hidden under the elytra. When the beetle is ready to fly, it spreads out the elytra and unfolds the hind wings, as in the picture above.

These protective front wings are so unique that they have given a name to the scientific order to which beetles belong. The name is **Coleoptera,** and it comes from two Greek works meaning "sheath wing."

THE PARTS OF A BEETLE'S BODY

A beetle's sheath wings are unique, but the rest of its body is much like that of other insects. The body is divided into three main parts: the head, thorax, and abdomen.

On the head are located the insect's mouth, eyes, and two important sense organs called antennae. The beetle's two pairs of wings and three pairs of legs are attached to the thorax. The abdomen contains the organs of respiration, digestion, and reproduction.

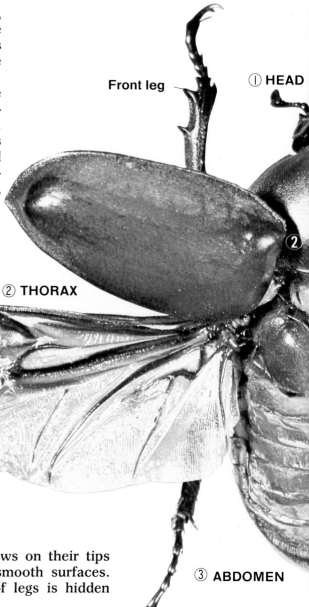

Front leg

① HEAD

②

② THORAX

③ ABDOMEN

A beetle's six legs have sharp claws on their tips that help the insect to cling to smooth surfaces. In this picture, the middle pair of legs is hidden behind the beetle's wings.

22

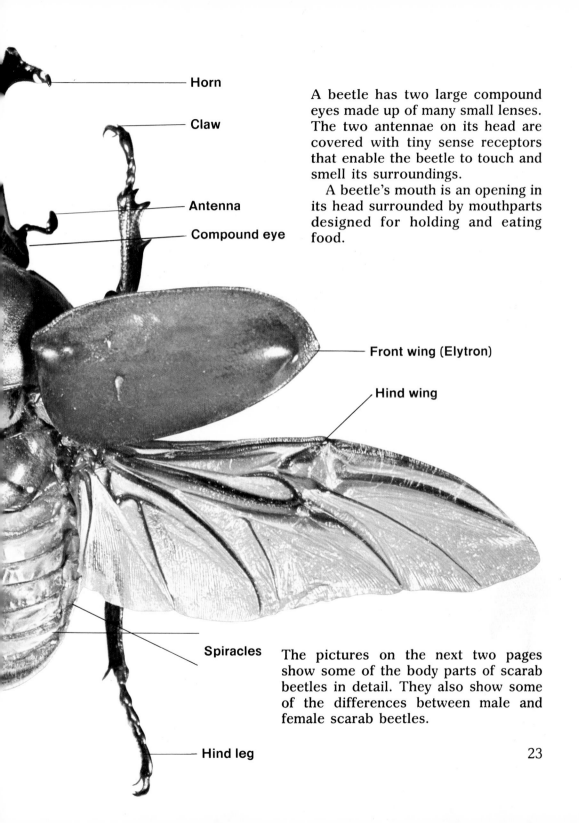

Horn

Claw

Antenna

Compound eye

Front wing (Elytron)

Hind wing

Spiracles

Hind leg

A beetle has two large compound eyes made up of many small lenses. The two antennae on its head are covered with tiny sense receptors that enable the beetle to touch and smell its surroundings.

A beetle's mouth is an opening in its head surrounded by mouthparts designed for holding and eating food.

The pictures on the next two pages show some of the body parts of scarab beetles in detail. They also show some of the differences between male and female scarab beetles.

23

A female scarab beetle

Many female scarab beetles have small bumps on their heads rather than well-developed horns.

The legs of a female scarab are covered with sharp spines.

A male scarab's spines are not as sharp or as numerous.

The antennae of scarab beetles have club-shaped segments on their tips.

A male scarab beetle

The mouthparts of this scarab species are used to suck sap from trees.

Adult beetles, like beetle larvae, take in air through spiracles on the sides of their bodies.

Opposite: **These beetles are feeding on sap oozing from a tree.**

In the picture on the opposite page, several kinds of scarab beetles can be seen on the trunk of a tree. With them is a stag beetle, recognized by its enormous curved mandibles, which look like the antlers of a male deer. (The white arrow points to the stag beetle.) All of these insects are busy feeding on the sweet sap oozing from the tree.

Tree sap is only one of the many different foods eaten by adult beetles. Large numbers of the insects are **herbivores,** feeding on the various parts of plants. Many kinds of beetles burrow through the bark of trees to eat the soft, nourishing tissue underneath. Others eat the flowers, leaves, stems, and roots of various green plants. These plant-eating beetles include such species as the boll weevil and the potato beetle, which do a great deal of damage to agricultural crops.

Other kinds of beetles eat animals rather than plants. Many of these beetles are **predators,** hunters that kill other animals to get their food. Most beetles prey on other insects, but some attack and eat snails, slugs, and worms. The diet of large water beetles includes tadpoles and even small fish.

Some beetles that eat the flesh of animals are not predators but **scavengers.** They feed on the bodies of animals that have died. Other beetle scavengers eat animal dung or dead plants. These insects play a useful role in removing such decaying material from the environment.

The insect shown here is a false blister beetle, one of the many kinds of beetles that feed on flowers. Some flower-eating beetles have mouthparts equipped with long tubes used to suck nectar. The false blister beetle uses its mandibles to eat flower pollen. This beetle got its common name because of its resemblance to another flower eater called the blister beetle. Many real blister beetles have a poison in their bodies that causes blisters and other skin irritations. False blister beetles don't share this characteristic. The scientific name of the false blister beetle family is Oedemeridae; true blister beetles belong to the family Meloidae.

These pictures show a horned scarab and a stag beetle fighting over the best feeding spot on a tree trunk. Male beetles of these two families use their horns and mandibles as weapons in battles over food or over mates. In the picture below, the horned beetle is using the long, forked horn on its head to push the stag beetle off the tree.

The scarab family (Scarabaeidae) is one of the largest in the order of beetles. Here is a family portrait of 15 different species of scarabs. Additional pictures and descriptions of some of these beetles appear on the following pages.

(4) *Chalcosoma atlas* is often called the giant beetle because of its large size. Its body, including the horns, is about 95 millimeters (mm) long. This species lives in Thailand, Burma, and other countries of Southeast Asia.

The scarabs shown here are part of a collection of beetles from many parts of the world. Their bodies have been preserved with chemicals and pinned to boards for display. This collection includes only scarabs with horns. Other scarab species lack horns, but most collectors do not find them as interesting as the horned varieties.

The beetles in these pictures are identified by their species names. These Latin names are recognized by all scientists no matter what language they speak. Common English names are also given for some species, but many of these exotic beetles have no common names in the English language. The sizes of the beetles are shown in millimeters, a metric unit used by scientists everywhere. (If you want to convert millimeters to inches, multiply by .04.)

(8) From Southeast Asia comes the elegant five-horned beetle *(Eupatorus gracilicornis)*. It measures 80 mm in length. (9) The white beetle *(Dynastes tityus)* lives in the southwestern part of the United States. (Body length 45 mm)

(1) This elephant beetle *(Megasoma elephas)* is found in Mexico and Central America. Its body length is 100 mm. (5) Native to Peru, *Heterogomphus hirtus* was given the last part of its name because of the thick hair on its body. *Hirtus* is a Latin word meaning "shaggy." (Body length 65 mm)

(7) *Golofa pizzaro* is a Central American species sometimes called a standing horn beetle. Its body length is about 65 mm. (10) *Scapanes australis* comes from the island of New Guinea in the South Pacific. *Australis,* a word meaning "southern," describes the geographic location of the beetle's home. (Body length 60 mm)

(11) Southeast Asia is the home of *Trichogomphus martabani.*
Members of this species measure about 50 mm in length.
(12) This brightly colored scarab, *Dynastes centaurus,* comes
from Central and West Africa. Like many beetles in the genus
Dynastes, it is large, measuring 80 mm in length.

(13) This jet-black scarab is commonly called the princess beetle.
Its scientific name is *Xylotrupes gideon,* and it lives in South
and Southeast Asia. (Body length 68 mm) (15) *Enema pan* is
one of the species often called rhinoceros beetles because of
their large horns. Its home is Mexico and South America, and
it measures about 50 mm in length.

Hercules beetles live in the tropical areas of Central America. Their bodies are often more than seven inches (180 mm) in length, including their long horns.

The scarab family includes the world's largest species of beetle, the giant hercules beetle *(Dynastes hercules),* pictured above. Members of this species often measure more than 180 mm from the tip of the horn to the end of the abdomen. The smallest beetles in the world belong to the family Ptiliidae. These beetles are usually less than 1 mm in length—not much bigger than the period at the end of this sentence.

In addition to the scarabs and the ptiliids, there are more than 150 other beetle families, each with its own special features. Let's take a look at representatives of some of these other groups...

Above: A tiger beetle. *Right:* The larva of a firefly feeding on a snail

Tiger beetles (left) are members of the family Cicindelidae. These beautifully striped insects are among the fiercest of the beetle predators. With the help of their keen eyesight, large wings, and strong legs, they can pursue and capture many kinds of insect prey.

The picture on the right shows the strangely shaped larva of a lightning bug or firefly, family Lampyridae. Like the adult beetles in this family, many lampyrid larvae have chemicals in their bodies that produce a flashing light. This characteristic has earned them the common name glowworms. The favorite prey of many glowworms are snails. A larva will reach into a snail shell and inject a substance into the inhabitant's soft body that turns it into liquid. Then the larva can easily suck its meal out of the shell.

This insect is sometimes called a jewel beetle because of its lovely shining colors.

The antennae of a longhorn beetle are often longer than the rest of the insect's body.

The beetle shown on the opposite page belongs to the family Buprestidae. Sometimes called jewel beetles, members of this group have metallic, jewel-like colors on their thoraxes and elytra. Another common name for one of these beetles is metallic wood borer, a name that describes the insect's living habits as well as its appearance. Female wood borers lay their eggs on tree bark. When the larvae hatch, they burrow through the bark and eat the soft tissue underneath.

The beetle shown in the picture above also spends its larval stage burrowing under tree bark. This white-striped insect belongs to a group commonly known as longhorn beetles because of their very long antennae. The family name of the longhorn beetle is Cerambycidae.

The large beetle shown below is just as fierce as its appearance suggests. It is a predaceous diving beetle, a member of the water beetle family Dytiscidae. The word **predaceous** comes from **predator,** and it describes this beetle's way of life. Both as larvae and as adults, diving beetles will try to kill and eat just about any small creature that comes near them.

Dytiscid beetles spend most of their time in ponds and pools, and they prey on animals that share their underwater environment. Adult diving beetles eat tadpoles and small fish as well as other water insects. The larvae of this family feed mainly on insects, seizing them with their very sharp mandibles.

Diving beetle larvae are such ferocious hunters that they have been given the nickname water tigers.

Both larvae and adults are specially equipped for underwater life. A dytiscid larva has special sacs inside its body that are used to store supplies of air taken in through its spiracles. An adult diving beetle stores extra air in a kind of pocket under its elytra. The adults of this family are expert swimmers, using their fringed, oar-shaped hind legs to row their way through the water. Diving beetle larvae can also swim, but they often use their six long legs to walk on the bottom of the ponds where they live.

41

Left: This picture shows another of the large water beetles in the family Dysticidae. The flat, streamlined shape of a dytiscid's body helps the beetle to glide smoothly through the water. Many members of this family are not only good swimmers but also skilled at flying. Their wings are strong, allowing the beetles to pursue prey in the air as well as underwater.

Right: Ladybugs, or ladybird beetles, belong to the family Coccinellidae. The ladybug in this picture has seven black spots on a red background, but other species have many different combinations of spots and background colors. These attractive little beetles are very helpful to human beings. The larvae and adults feed on destructive insects like the tiny green aphids shown in the picture. An adult ladybug can eat as many as 60 aphids a day; some larvae may devour 500 of the insects in a single day!

Left: Beetles in the family Carabidae are also famous for their large appetites. Commonly called ground beetles, these insects are often seen moving rapidly over the ground in search of prey. The beetle shown here feeds on snails, like many of its relatives. Its head and thorax are thin and flexible, enabling the beetle to reach into the protective shell and pull out the soft body of the snail inside.

Right: This spotted beetle belongs to the very large family Chrysomelidae. Members of this family feed on all kinds of plants, and some do a great deal of damage to crops. The Colorado potato beetle is probably the most unpopular of the Chrysomelidae. Both the larvae and the adults of this species have enormous appetites for the leaves of potato plants. The beetle pictured here enjoys a diet of tender willow leaves.

Left: Like most male members of the family Lucanidae, this beetle has huge, pronged mandibles that look very much like the antlers of stags, or male deer. The mandibles of female stag beetles are not any bigger than those of other beetle families. Male stag beetles use their mandibles as weapons in battles, just as male deer use their antlers. They fight with each other over feeding territories or over females of their species at mating time.

Right: This dull gray beetle has one distinctive feature — a very long beak or snout on the front of its head. Commonly called a snout beetle, it is a member of the family Curculionidae. Snout beetles are herbivores, and the favorite foods of some species are plants cultivated by human beings. The boll weevil is a snout beetle that eats various parts of cotton plants as a larva and an adult. Other snout beetles cause damage by feeding on stored grain products such as wheat and rice.

44

Left: The shiny green beetle shown here is one of the hornless members of the family Scarabaeidae. It is part of a group commonly known as leaf chafers, beetles that eat the leaves, flowers, and roots of green plants. One species in this group, the Japanese beetle, did tremendous damage to plants in the eastern United States during the early 1900s. Brought by accident from Japan, the beetle multiplied rapidly because it had no natural enemies in North America. To control its spread, scientists had to import predators and parasites from the beetle's homeland.

Right: This beautifully marked beetle is another carabid, a member of the ground beetle family Carabidae. Like all its relatives, it is a skillful hunter, feeding on insects, snails, and worms. The species shown here spends all its time on the ground because its hind wings are so undeveloped that it cannot fly at all. Like most ground beetles, it can run very rapidly with the help of its long, thin legs.

45

GLOSSARY

antennae (an-TEN-ee)—sense organs on the heads of insects, used for smelling and touching. The singular form of the word is **antenna,** pronounced an-TEN-uh.

Coleoptera (ko-lee-AHP-tuh-ruh)—the scientific order to which beetles belong

elytra (eh-LIE-truh)—the hard front wings of beetles, which serve as covers for the hind wings. The singular form of the word is **elytron.**

grub—a special name for the larva of a beetle

herbivore (ER-bih-vor)—an animal that eats only plants

larva—the second stage of metamorphosis, in which the insect is wingless and wormlike. The plural form of the word is **larvae,** pronounced LAR-vee.

mandibles (MAN-dih-buhls)—insect mouthparts used to hold and bite food

metamorphosis (met-uh-MOR-fuh-sis)—the process of development that produces an adult beetle. During metamorphosis, the insect goes through four complete changes in form: egg, larva, pupa, adult.

molting—shedding an old skin to make way for a new one

predaceous (preh-DAY-shus)—living by preying on other animals

predator—an animal that kills and eats other animals

pupa (PEW-puh)—the third stage of metamorphosis, during which the larva changes into an adult beetle. The plural form of the word is **pupae,** pronounced PEW-pee.

scavenger (SCAV-uhn-jur)—an animal that eats the bodies of dead animals or decaying plant material

spiracles (SPEAR-uh-kuhls)—breathing holes on an insect's body

FAMILIES OF BEETLES

Scientists have identified and named about 250,000 individual *species,* or kinds, of beetles. The species are classified in groups based on the similarities that exist among them. A *genus* is made up of several closely related species. A beetle *family* is an even larger group consisting of many *genera* (the Latin plural of *genus*).

There are at least 150 families in the order of beetles. Here is a list of the families mentioned in this book and the pages on which they appear:

INDEX